The Time Traveller Book of KNIGHTS and CASTLES

Judy Hindley

Illustrated by Toni Goffe
Designed by John Jamieson

Contents

The People You Will Meet in This Book

Everyone you will meet in this book has special duties and work to do. People are born with these duties, and have little chance to change their way of life.

This is mainly because life for these people is hard and dangerous—like life on a ship or in an army. The comfort and safety of each person depends on the work of all the others.

For example, there must be strong leaders, like Baron Godfrey, to protect people from enemies and criminals. But the baron needs his people, too— to work and fight for him.

Everyone must obey God and the king. God is obeyed through his Church, which has its own leaders. The Church's ruler is the Pope.

SIMON, KNIGHT

TROUBADOUR

A knight is a fighting man with special privileges. You can become a knight by training as a squire or by showing great skill and bravery in battle. Some knights are also poets and musicians, like the travelling minstrels. These knights are called troubadours.

ROBERT, SQUIRE

A squire must be of noble birth—the son of another knight, or someone with a title, such as baron. He is a trainee-knight.

MAN-AT-ARMS

A man-at-arms has the arms and equipment of a knight, but not the title of knight.

FOOT SOLDIER

A foot-soldier is a fighting man who is not of noble birth. Knights always fight on horseback.

2

BARON GODFREY   LADY ALICE

Baron Godfrey is a knight and a nobleman. He owns land. His job is to protect his land and people, and to see that his people live peacefully together, keeping the laws. He is the lord of many less powerful knights.

BISHOP

PRIEST

A priest is the religious leader of the people in his parish. His lord is the bishop, who has many parishes and a great church called a cathedral.

FRIAR

A friar is a priest without a parish. Friars travel about, trying to serve God by teaching and preaching.

NUN →   MONK

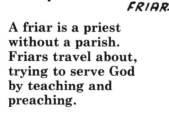

Monks and nuns are people who have promised to serve God by work and prayer, and sometimes by teaching and helping people.

Each lady must obey her husband, or her father if she is not married, as well as her king.

LADY ANNA

Many noble ladies live in the castle. Lady Alice gives them a home and helps teach the young girls. In return they help and obey her.

STEWARD

A steward is a head servant. Some can read and write a bit, and do large sums. Few other people can.

SERVANT →

Servants must obey the people they work for. They live in the houses or castles of their masters.

PEASANT

Peasants belong to the land of a certain lord. They may not leave it. The lord may let them farm some of it for themselves, in return for the work they do for him.

SERFS →

Serfs are slaves. Many are the children of foreigners who were captured in wars and sold to the rich.

Going Back in Time

The people you have just met are not real people – at least, as far as we know. But all the things they do are things real people have done. All over Europe you can see the castles they lived in. In museums you can find some of the actual furniture they used, and pictures of people taking baths and playing with pets just like the people in this book.

But museums cannot often show everything you want to see, all in one place. And real castles are often half-destroyed, and empty. You may often have wished you could go back in time to see how a castle looked when the fire was roaring on the hearth, and the tapestries were bright, and people were talking and laughing in the candle-light.

We have invented a magic time helmet to help you make this trip. Below you can see how it works.

Put on the Helmet

Here is the magic Time helmet. You can set the 'Place' and 'Time' dials to go back in time to any place you like. There are lots of gadgets for emergencies. All you have to do is pick your destination.

Pick Your Destination

We know there were lots of castles in Northwest Europe in about 1240. And we know this was a great time for knightly deeds and adventures. So let us set the 'Place' dial for this bit—and let us start going back.

Our first stop is in 1940, at about the time your mum and dad were born. Notice the big, funny-looking radio.

Now we have gone back another forty years. Perhaps your great-grandfather is a teenager now. A lot of things are different.

Now we have jumped a century. Houses are heated by log fires and lit by candles, and many families go to bed early to save fuel.

We have really come a long way, now. Even books are a luxury. We are almost on the last lap of our journey—turn the page, and see.

3

Journey to a Castle

You are in Europe in the year 1240. You find yourself in rough, dangerous country. Long ago, the Romans built roads and cities here. But most of the Romans left 600 years ago, and often their cities crumbled. The biggest buildings you see now are cathedrals, and the great castles built by the kings and fighting barons.

The countries of Europe are not like those you know. They have different names and languages. They hardly seem like countries—few have really strong kings and governments.

All over Europe, powerful barons are fighting each other for land. Each tries to gather as many knights as he can, and build the strongest castle. He rules over all his land.

The peasants in this village cannot leave Baron Godfrey's land—unless they grow rich enough to buy their freedom, or brave enough to escape to a big town.

This is one of the first kinds of machine. The stream turns the wheel and the axle of the wheel turns a stone inside the hut. The heavy stone grinds wheat into flour.

WATERMILL

AXLE

Animals and people still do many kinds of hard work—like this farmer and his oxen.

Over the last two centuries, many thousands of watermills have been built. They do lots of work that used to be done by serfs. The whole country is a little bit richer now.

Baron Godfrey owns several castles, miles apart. He and his family, knights and servants eat the food grown on the castle lands. When it runs out, they move on.

TAPESTRIES

BARON GODFREY

BEST CANDLESTICKS

Baron Godfrey takes everything valuable with him, in case his castle is conquered while he is gone. He takes food for the journey too. The carts only travel about 30 km a day.

How We Know What a Time

We have lots of clues to help us work out how people lived in the past. We can still see many of their writings, buildings and tools—and pictures they painted, like those above.

4

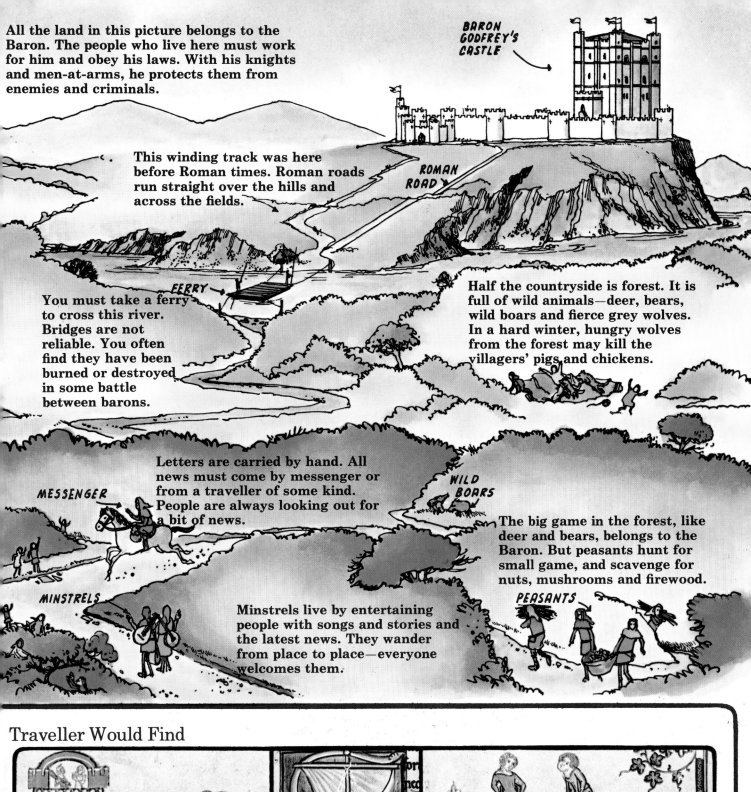

All the land in this picture belongs to the Baron. The people who live here must work for him and obey his laws. With his knights and men-at-arms, he protects them from enemies and criminals.

BARON GODFREY'S CASTLE

This winding track was here before Roman times. Roman roads run straight over the hills and across the fields.

ROMAN ROAD

FERRY

You must take a ferry to cross this river. Bridges are not reliable. You often find they have been burned or destroyed in some battle between barons.

Half the countryside is forest. It is full of wild animals—deer, bears, wild boars and fierce grey wolves. In a hard winter, hungry wolves from the forest may kill the villagers' pigs and chickens.

Letters are carried by hand. All news must come by messenger or from a traveller of some kind. People are always looking out for a bit of news.

MESSENGER

WILD BOARS

The big game in the forest, like deer and bears, belongs to the Baron. But peasants hunt for small game, and scavenge for nuts, mushrooms and firewood.

MINSTRELS

Minstrels live by entertaining people with songs and stories and the latest news. They wander from place to place—everyone welcomes them.

PEASANTS

Traveller Would Find

However, there are still many mysteries and missing clues. Historians are people who work at solving these mysteries. We had to ask several historians for help with this book.

History is like a detective story that never really ends. New clues are always being discovered, and new ideas about what the clues might mean.

Perhaps you, one day, will find a new clue, or a new solution to one of the puzzles of history. 'Going Further', on page 32, tells more about what to read and what to look for.

Beyond the Castle Walls

Baron Godfrey's castle is very strong. It is almost impossible for an enemy to get in. Behind the wall at the back is a steep cliff. Round the front and sides are a deep ditch and two rows of heavily defended walls. The entrance is like an obstacle course—the pictures below show how difficult it is to get through it.

What you find beyond the gates is almost a little town. The castle has its own carpenters and its own thatchers and masons to keep the thatched roofs and stone walls repaired. It has shoemakers and blacksmiths, tailors and armourers. There are stables, water, food supplies—even a fishpond. If you were besieged you might live here quite comfortably for weeks.

Archers patrol these thick walls, ready to shoot enemies trying to cross the ditch. They stand behind the top bit of wall and shoot through the slits in it.

DOOR TO WALL WALK

DOVE COTE

TURRET

WALL WALK

BOARS KEPT FOR AMUSEMENT

HAY STACKS

DOG KENNELS

MEWS WHERE FALCONS ARE KEPT

HUTS FOR SERVANTS

DITCH

GATEHOUSE

DOUBLE DOOR

PORTCULLIS

BARBICAN

DRAWBRIDGE

BEGGARS

A barbican is an extra gatehouse outside the ditch.

Through the Gates

DRAWBRIDGE IS LOWERED

GATE OF BARBICAN

First you have to get through the barbican. This is to stop enemies from coming up to the entrance. (They might fill up the ditch.)

6

Sentries patrolling the walkway behind the battlements can see for miles. But the wind can be bitter cold, so there are sentry-boxes to shelter them, and sometimes ovens to keep their food warm.

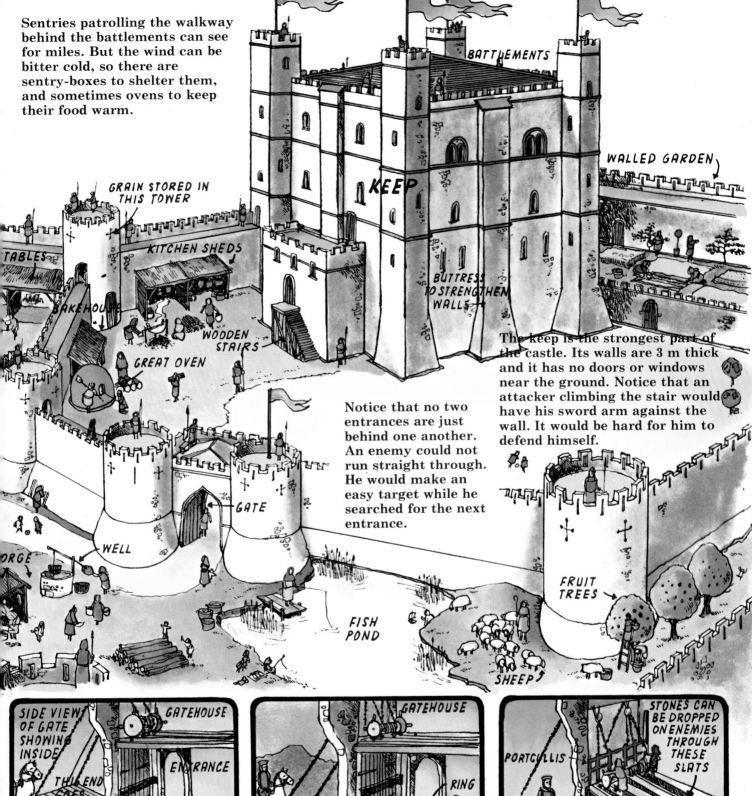

BATTLEMENTS

KEEP

WALLED GARDEN

GRAIN STORED IN THIS TOWER

TABLES

KITCHEN SHEDS

BAKEHOUSE

WOODEN STAIRS

GREAT OVEN

BUTTRESS TO STRENGTHEN WALLS

The keep is the strongest part of the castle. Its walls are 3 m thick and it has no doors or windows near the ground. Notice that an attacker climbing the stair would have his sword arm against the wall. It would be hard for him to defend himself.

Notice that no two entrances are just behind one another. An enemy could not run straight through. He would make an easy target while he searched for the next entrance.

GATE

WELL

FORGE

FRUIT TREES

FISH POND

SHEEP

SIDE VIEW OF GATE SHOWING INSIDE

GATEHOUSE

ENTRANCE

THIS END GOES DOWN

THIS GOES UP

PIT

GATEHOUSE

RING

PIT

BOLT

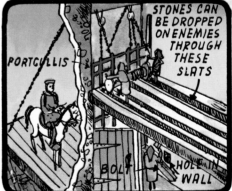

STONES CAN BE DROPPED ON ENEMIES THROUGH THESE SLATS

PORTCULLIS

BOLT

HOLE IN WALL

Now the drawbridge is lowered. One end lifts up from a pit below the entrance floor. The other end swings down to make a bridge. This picture shows how.

Now the drawbridge is bolted into place. The entrance is still defended by an iron grill called a portcullis, and big double doors.

Now the portcullis is raised. It slides up grooves in the walls. The doors are unbolted. You can see these grooves and bolt-holes in many castles.

7

Inside the Keep

The keep is where the baron's family lives, together with knights, men-at-arms, servants and friends.

This keep was built two hundred years ago—about 1040. Then it was a draughty, cold and gloomy place. Many young squires died coughing. But now it is much more comfortable and cheerful. The walls are hung with rugs from crusader lands, there is glass in some of the windows, and the fireplaces give more heat and less smoke.

The courtyard round the keep is thronged with travellers—pilgrims, pedlars, traders, and the barefoot friars who wander Europe teaching and preaching.

In the upper rooms of the keep women sew, weave and embroider, listening to the songs and poems of troubadours. Sometimes the friars read to them and even bring them the latest teachings on philosophy and science. A few of these women are among the best-educated people in Europe. Some become troubadours themselves, like the famous Marie de France.

THIS LADY IS WEAVING A TAPESTRY

Notice the direction in which stair curves. This helps people defend the tower. An attacker climbing up would find it very hard to use his sword.

"Peace, oh my stricken lute"

TROUBADOUR

THATCHER REPAIRING ROOF

KITCHEN SHEDS

BARON

One of the steward's jobs is to settle quarrels and punish criminals. Baron Godfrey's stewards and bailiffs are his police.

DUNGEON

SALT MERCHANT

STEWARD

HE STOLE MY PIG.

IT'S MY PIG!

Meat can be kept through the winter if it is salted or pickled with spices. You can get salt from sea-water, but many spices come only from certain countries. They are so important people fight wars about them.

PILGRIM

FRIAR

8

Maids look after Lady Alice's babies and children while Lady Alice looks after the rest of the castle people.

In her garden, Lady Alice has mint, thyme, fennel, parsley, sage and hyssop to use for cooking and medicine. But she says, 'The best doctors are Dr. Quiet, Dr. Merry and Dr. Diet.'

People believe that some herbs should be planted, gathered and swallowed under certain stars. If parsley is planted on Good Friday, it is supposed to cure sick fish.

MAIDS

BARON'S BEDROOM

GARDEROBE

CHAPLAIN

CHAPEL

Tiny rooms and cupboards and passages are cut into these thick outer walls. The garderobe is a lavatory. It has no plumbing—just a hole going down through the wall.

GREAT HALL

BEAMS

These fireplaces have short chimneys which go through the wall instead of up to the roof. They can make the rooms very smoky if the wind blows from the wrong direction.

VAULTED BASEMENT

STOREROOM

Pork, timber, game, corn, bacon, cheese and many other supplies come from the lord's own land.

Stocks of food are kept here for emergencies. Precious things like spices and sugar are stored here, too. It is a bit like a shop. Records are kept of whatever goes in or out.

WHAT'S THE NEWS?

The castle people make their own soap. They save up the laundry and do a lot at once, boiling it in cauldrons and hanging it to dry like this.

9

Dawn at the Castle

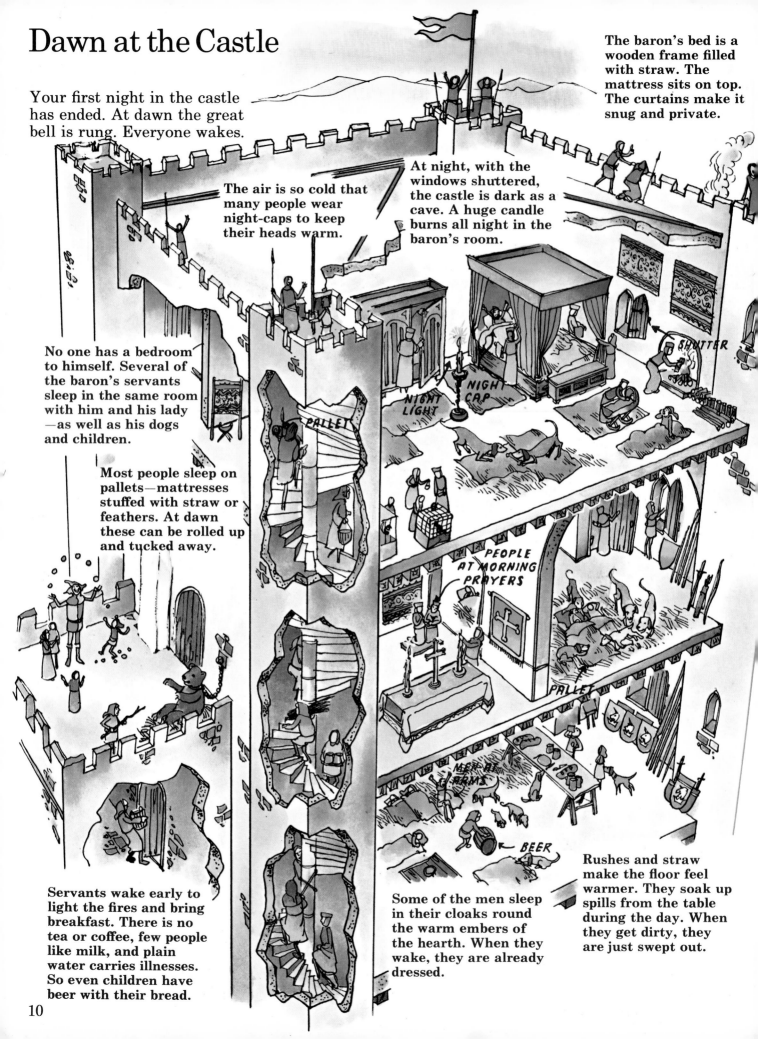

Your first night in the castle has ended. At dawn the great bell is rung. Everyone wakes.

The air is so cold that many people wear night-caps to keep their heads warm.

At night, with the windows shuttered, the castle is dark as a cave. A huge candle burns all night in the baron's room.

The baron's bed is a wooden frame filled with straw. The mattress sits on top. The curtains make it snug and private.

No one has a bedroom to himself. Several of the baron's servants sleep in the same room with him and his lady —as well as his dogs and children.

Most people sleep on pallets—mattresses stuffed with straw or feathers. At dawn these can be rolled up and tucked away.

Servants wake early to light the fires and bring breakfast. There is no tea or coffee, few people like milk, and plain water carries illnesses. So even children have beer with their bread.

Some of the men sleep in their cloaks round the warm embers of the hearth. When they wake, they are already dressed.

Rushes and straw make the floor feel warmer. They soak up spills from the table during the day. When they get dirty, they are just swept out.

PALLET

NIGHT LIGHT

NIGHT CAP

SHUTTER

PEOPLE AT MORNING PRAYERS

PALLET

MEN-AT-ARMS

BEER

Baron Godfrey Gets Dressed

BEFORE HE GETS UP HE PUTS ON HIS SHIRT.

HE SHAVES BY RUBBING HIS WHISKERS OFF WITH A ROUGH PUMICE STONE.

HE IS HELPED ON WITH HIS LONG HOSE.

HIS SHOES FASTEN UP WITH A BUTTON.

HIS ROBE IS LINED WITH FUR.

A USEFUL BAG SLIDES ONTO HIS BELT.

Lady Alice Gets Dressed

SHE WEARS A TUNIC

AND ROBE CALLED A SURCOAT.

HER HAIR IS BRAIDED

COILED ROUND HER EARS

COVERED WITH A BAND OF CLOTH

AND TOPPED OFF WITH A HAT.

And Others Get Dressed

MONKS AND NUNS SPEND THEIR LIVES HELPING PEOPLE AND SERVING GOD.

THEIR LONG ROBES SHOW THEY ARE SPECIAL.

GIRLS WEAR THEIR HAIR LOOSE, BUT DRESS JUST LIKE THEIR MOTHERS.

BOYS DRESS LIKE THEIR FATHERS— THEY EVEN CARRY DAGGERS IN THEIR BELTS.

WORKERS AND SERVANTS WEAR SENSIBLE, TOUGH CLOTHES.

ON WET DAYS, WORKING PEOPLE WEAR CLOGS TO KEEP THEIR FEET DRY.

Taking a Bath

IT TAKES A LONG TIME TO HEAT ENOUGH BUCKETS OF WATER TO FILL A BATH. BECAUSE OF THIS PEOPLE OFTEN SHARE A BATH.

Baths are mostly for fun—or before a feast. Servants bring in a wooden tub and fill it with hot water. Since the soap does not smell very nice, they sprinkle the water with herbs and flowers.

THE SOAP IS MADE OF MUTTON FAT, WOOD ASH AND SODA. IT IS SOFT AND SQUISHY.

FLOWERS
HERBS
BOWL OF SOAP
HANDLES FOR CARRYING
THE TUB HAS HANDLES SO IT CAN BE CARRIED ROUND. IT HAS TO BE FILLED AND EMPTIED BY BUCKETS AND BAILERS.
BELLOWS TO MAKE FIRE BURN

Going on a Hunt

Baron Godfrey spends much of his life making war on enemy barons. His knights and men-at-arms must be well trained and always ready for battle. The knights practise fighting by having jousts and tournaments, which you can read about on pages 24 and 25. In good weather they spend the rest of their time in the woods and fields, riding with hounds and hawks.

These pages show how their sporting animals are trained, and how they hunt. There are great arguments between huntsmen and falconers over whether hounds or hawks are the most brave and noble company. In the evenings, their stories are told round the fire after splendid feasts of wild boar and venison.

The peasants and country people do not share this sport. Their fields and crops may be ruined by the hunt. They may be forced to give refreshment to the hunters from their own small supplies of food. And they themselves are not allowed to touch Baron Godfrey's game. These pages show some of their story, too.

Hunting a Stag

The spring seems very lovely when you have been shut inside through the long winter months. People sing and make music as they ride.

Soon the hounds will pick up the scent of game. Then the chase will begin . . . and no one knows where it will lead.

If you were April's lady And I were lord of May

Ladies ride with the hunt, singing and gossiping, their falcons on their wrists.

PEASANTS

These peasants are terrified by the sound of the hunt. They are poaching—hunting the baron's game. If caught, they will be punished.

TRAINING A FALCON

This is how falcons used to be trained. Today, Falcons are protected birds. It is **against the law** to steal eggs or baby birds.

* STRICTLY FORBIDDEN TODAY

KEEP THE BIRD IN A SAFE QUIET PLACE AT FIRST. FEED IT BY HAND SO THAT IT GETS TO KNOW YOU. WEAR A SPECIAL TOUGH GLOVE, SO IT CAN PERCH ON YOUR WRIST.

HOOD

BELL

WHEN THE BIRD IS TAME, PUT A LITTLE BELL ON ITS FOOT, AND LEASH IT. USE A HOOD TO KEEP IT CALM AND QUIET. THEN YOU CAN TAKE IT OUT FOR THE FIRST TIME.

Hounds and Their Kennels

Every day the kennel is swept and sprinkled with fresh straw.

The keeper of the hounds is paid a half penny a day besides his food and lodging. It is a good job, although he will have to save for eight days to buy a fur hat.

The hounds are treated much more gently than children. One of the stable boys sleeps in the kennel with them, to keep them calm during the night.

The huntsmen have chased for hours, through dense forest and brambles, and over ditches. They are tired, muddy and sore. But the horn leads them on.

This hunting horn is made from a stag's antler. It only plays one note. But the master of the hunt can signal by long and short blasts on it.

It has been a good hunt. The hounds were fast and fierce and cunning, and the stag ran hard. Music is played to honour the dying stag.

BEGIN BY LETTING THE FALCON FLY SHORT DISTANCES, ON ITS LEASH. WHISTLE IT BACK TO YOU—THEN REWARD IT WITH FOOD. BUT DO NOT OVERFEED IT.

WHEN IT IS FULLY TRAINED, TAKE IT OFF THE LEASH. IT WILL LEARN TO HUNT BY ITSELF. WATCH IT CAREFULLY. AFTER A WHILE YOU WILL SEE IT DIVE ON ITS PREY.

THE SOUND OF THE FALCON'S BELL WILL LEAD YOU TO IT THROUGH THE UNDERGROWTH. WHEN YOU TAKE IT AWAY FROM ITS PREY, ALWAYS REWARD YOUR BIRD WITH A BIT OF THE RAW MEAT.

Having a Feast

The 'kitchen' is just a group of sheds in the courtyard. Servants have been working here since dawn.

Spices and herbs must be ground up with a mortar and pestle. Lots of spices are used, to hide the taste of the meat. Without refrigerators, it goes bad quickly.

Much of the meat is roasted on spits in front of the fire. The servant boy who has to turn this spit is using an old, wet archery target as a fire screen.

There is no butter. Meat dripping is used instead.

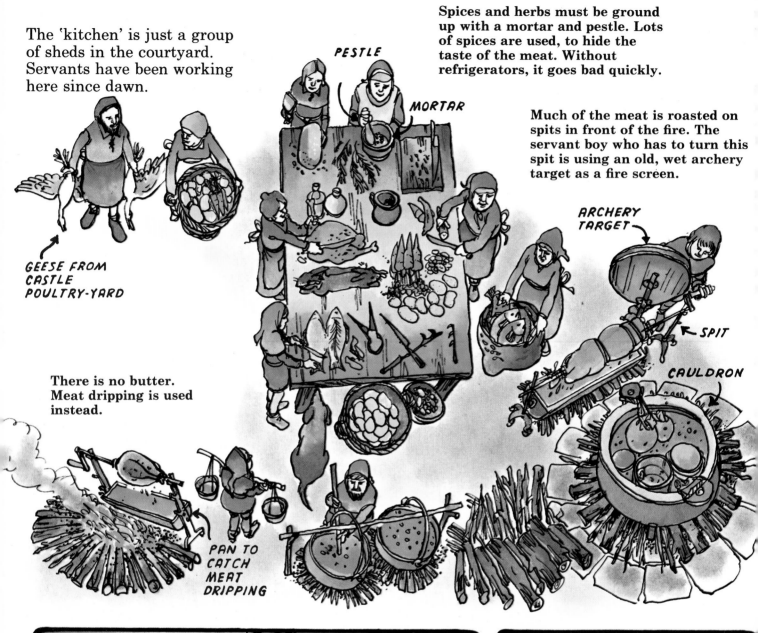

GEESE FROM CASTLE POULTRY-YARD

PESTLE

MORTAR

ARCHERY TARGET

SPIT

CAULDRON

PAN TO CATCH MEAT DRIPPING

Baking Bread

A fire is lit inside the oven to heat it while the dough is being made. Then the fire is raked out and the dough popped in, to bake as the oven cools.

Every bit of precious heat is used. After the bread is baked, the oven will be used for many other things, from making cakes to drying feathers and fuel.

Inside a Cauldron

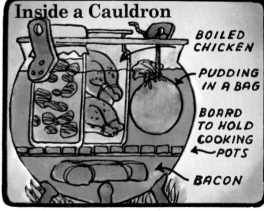

BOILED CHICKEN

PUDDING IN A BAG

BOARD TO HOLD COOKING POTS

BACON

Here are some of the things that might be cooked all together in a cauldron. Later the hot water will be used for washing up. Nothing will be wasted.

Sometimes food is scarce. In the winter, even rich people may live on beans and porridge. The poor often go hungry. During a famine some years ago they ate grass.

But at noon, in the great hall, the tables are always laid as well as possible. Baron Godfrey invites everyone—minstrels, traders, wandering knights. This is how he gets news of the world and keeps his friends. Everyone loves the music, games and stories.

It is late summer now, and the food is splendid. There will be four courses today, each with soup, fish, meat and sweets. Here are some of the dishes:

Boar's head with brawn pudding
Shellfish scented with jasmine, rosemary and marigold
Fruit tarts
Salmon with orange
Beef with spices
Sugared nuts
Stuffed quarter of bear
Sugared mackerel
Squirrel stew
Apples and figs
Cakes with honey

Only the baron and Lady Alice (and perhaps some of their fine guests) have chairs. They sit at a special raised table— the 'high table'. The other tables are just boards resting on trestles.

Eating a Meal

You must wash your hands before meals, since you eat with your fingers. Squires bring basins and pitchers to the fine people. The others use basins near the door.

Very few people use plates. One of the young squires serving at table will cut a slice of stale bread for you to put your food on. Later these will be given to the poor.

You use your own knife to cut up your meat. A platter of food is shared by two people, and usually you share a cup, too. You make friends quickly, this way.

Trip to a Building Site

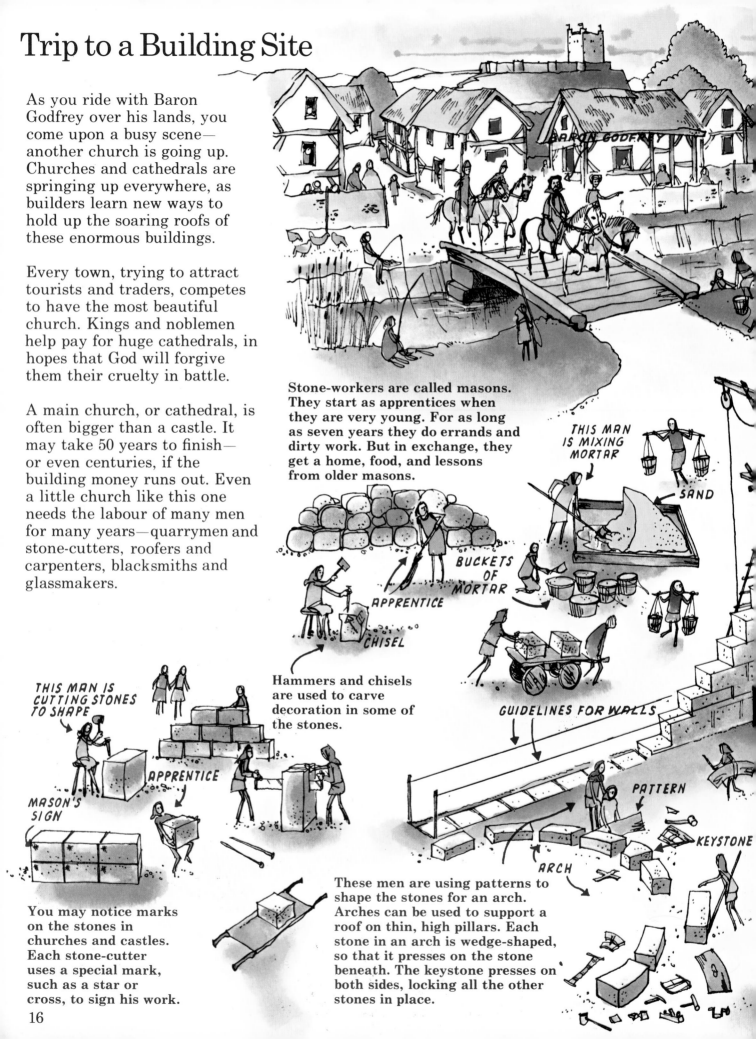

As you ride with Baron Godfrey over his lands, you come upon a busy scene— another church is going up. Churches and cathedrals are springing up everywhere, as builders learn new ways to hold up the soaring roofs of these enormous buildings.

Every town, trying to attract tourists and traders, competes to have the most beautiful church. Kings and noblemen help pay for huge cathedrals, in hopes that God will forgive them their cruelty in battle.

A main church, or cathedral, is often bigger than a castle. It may take 50 years to finish— or even centuries, if the building money runs out. Even a little church like this one needs the labour of many men for many years—quarrymen and stone-cutters, roofers and carpenters, blacksmiths and glassmakers.

Stone-workers are called masons. They start as apprentices when they are very young. For as long as seven years they do errands and dirty work. But in exchange, they get a home, food, and lessons from older masons.

THIS MAN IS MIXING MORTAR

SAND

BUCKETS OF MORTAR

APPRENTICE

CHISEL

Hammers and chisels are used to carve decoration in some of the stones.

GUIDELINES FOR WALLS

THIS MAN IS CUTTING STONES TO SHAPE

APPRENTICE

MASON'S SIGN

PATTERN

KEYSTONE

ARCH

You may notice marks on the stones in churches and castles. Each stone-cutter uses a special mark, such as a star or cross, to sign his work.

These men are using patterns to shape the stones for an arch. Arches can be used to support a roof on thin, high pillars. Each stone in an arch is wedge-shaped, so that it presses on the stone beneath. The keystone presses on both sides, locking all the other stones in place.

16

This workman is nailing wooden slats on to the timber frame of the roof. Later this roof will be covered with tiles or lead sheets.

Water is needed for making mortar. Mortar is a mixture of sand, water and lime, which is used to stick the stones of a building together. It dries very hard.

PULLEY

TREADMILL

These men are using mortar to stick the stones together. They build scaffolding to stand on as the walls get high.

ARCH

KEYSTONE

PILLAR

Almost everything must be done by hand. Lifting the heavy stones is very hard work. One man has to turn by foot the wheel that pulls the rope that lifts the buckets of stone.

Beneath these walls is another set of walls, reaching deep underground. These foundations will give solid support to the heavy building.

Several of the men you see here may be foreigners. Lots of master masons have wander-years—a time when they travel round to see new ways of working.

A Trip to Town

Baron Godfrey's steward is off to town. Lady Alice has made a huge shopping list. She is giving a feast and she needs plenty of good wax candles and some special red dye for her new dress—as well as spices, silks, new sword blades, and other things that come from foreign countries.

The steward is delighted to go. The town is very exciting. Thirty years ago it was just a cross-roads with a little market and a huddle of houses. All the land nearby belonged to Lord John (commonly known as John Deadtooth). But John needed money to go on a crusade, so he rented the land to some thrifty merchants and craftsmen. Look what has happened since.

CRIMINALS ARE HANGED HERE

People like goldsmiths, who have learned a craft, belong to a kind of club called a guild. Its members take care of one another. They have their own slang, badges and songs, as well as special signs and customs, like the knights. They try to keep their craft a mystery.

These birds help collect the town rubbish. (The pigs and dogs in the streets help, too.) The rubbishy streets stink— but just beyond the gates are woods and fields.

GUILDHALL

PILLORY

HOSPITAL 'HOTEL-DE-DIEU' WHERE NUNS LOOK AFTER POOR, SICK PEOPLE

Each town has its own laws and punishments. In one town you can be put in the pillory if you sell stinking fish or pretend to be a holy hermit to get food.

This is one of the first shops you see. The barber is also the dentist and the surgeon. He pulls teeth and he treats the sick by cutting them to make them bleed a little, into a bowl.

BARBER'S SHOP

GOLDSMITH'S SHOP

At night, the gatekeeper shuts these gates to keep out ruffians. Then watchmen walk the dark streets with lanterns, crying the curfew. This means that people must 'cover' their fires—flimsy houses catch fire easily.

GATES

The goldsmith's shop is the bank. It is well-protected (because of the gold) so it is a safe place to leave money.

18

BARON GODFREY'S STEWARD

The church is always busy. Merchants meet here and sometimes bible plays are acted on the porch. People come to gossip as well as pray—and to see the story-pictures inside. A hunted criminal is safe from arrest if he stays near the altar.

OLD SQUIRE WOUNDED IN BATTLE

POND

TOWN SQUARE

WATERING TROUGH

MARKET STALLS

PICK-POCKET AT WORK

ESCAPING PEASANT

This peasant is running away from Lord John. He hopes to become an apprentice and learn a trade. If he stays in the town for a year and a day he will be a free man.

RICH MEN HAVE THEIR OWN 'POLICE'

Each market stall must buy a licence from the town council. This is one of the ways the council gets money. The council is a group of important townspeople who make laws and deal with things like fire protection.

This pilgrim is travelling to a saint's tomb. Then, he hopes, God will forgive his sins. You can tell he is a pilgrim by the cross he wears.

PILGRIM

PEOPLE ARE VERY FOND OF THEIR GARDENS

TEACHER

PILGRIM

The first universities started like this—just a few good teachers, selling knowledge. The lectures are in Latin, and people come to them from all over Europe.

Italian bankers are well-known for lending money as well as keeping it safe. They charge the borrower, and pay the lender for the use of the money. Of course, they take a bit extra for their trouble. The extra charges are called 'interest'.

MONEY LENDERS

Many Jews become money-lenders, because the Christian laws do not allow them to do much else. Some become very rich, which makes people jealous.

This river is the town's main water supply.

19

The Training of a Knight

You will notice lots of children round the castle. One of them is the baron's nephew, Robert. Like many boys of noble birth, Robert was sent to live with his uncle when he was very young—about six years old.

For many years, Robert served as a page, learning to be courteous and obedient. When he became a squire, at 14, he began training to be a knight.

His cousin, Simon, is about to take his knightly vows. Turn the page and see.

Learning About Armour

Robert helps his lord dress, and arms him for jousts and battles.

This teaches him how to use armour and look after it.

Archery Lessons

LOADING A CROSSBOW

Almost everyone learns to use a bow and arrow. Skilful hunters are always needed, particularly in winter, when food is scarce.

All the people in the castle love to hunt. But knights never use their cross-bows in a battle. They always fight man-to-man.

Riding Practice

Robert has to learn to ride one-handed, to keep his weapon arm free. He must train his horse to get used to noise—or it might bolt during a battle.

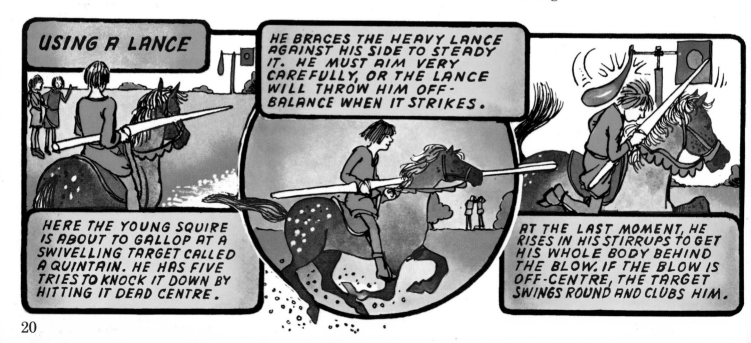

USING A LANCE

HE BRACES THE HEAVY LANCE AGAINST HIS SIDE TO STEADY IT. HE MUST AIM VERY CAREFULLY, OR THE LANCE WILL THROW HIM OFF-BALANCE WHEN IT STRIKES.

HERE THE YOUNG SQUIRE IS ABOUT TO GALLOP AT A SWIVELLING TARGET CALLED A QUINTAIN. HE HAS FIVE TRIES TO KNOCK IT DOWN BY HITTING IT DEAD CENTRE.

AT THE LAST MOMENT, HE RISES IN HIS STIRRUPS TO GET HIS WHOLE BODY BEHIND THE BLOW. IF THE BLOW IS OFF-CENTRE, THE TARGET SWINGS ROUND AND CLUBS HIM.

He cleans rusty mail armour by rolling it in a barrel of sand.

ABACUS (COUNTING STICKS)

The castle priest teaches Robert to read and write a little. Sometimes Lady Alice reads to him, and tells him stories of brave and famous people.

There is little paper, so he and his friends use pointed sticks and waxed tablets to practise writing. They need an abacus to do sums with Roman numerals.

Sword Practice

Young boys use small, blunt swords or even wooden ones, and little round shields called bucklers. They slash with the sword's edge, catching blows with the sword or the buckler.

As the boys get stronger they use heavier weapons. The sharp-edged battle sword weighs about 1½kg. It can slice through armour, cutting off arms and legs.

Games

While the knights practise jousting, the squires wrestle and fight and 'joust' with wooden sticks and horses.

When knights and older squires come round, the small boys must be ready for a rough time. No one is very gentle—a knight must learn to be tough.

A Squire Becomes a Knight

The time has come for Simon to be dubbed a knight. Several of his friends will be knighted with him. Tomorrow, after the ceremony, there will be feasts and jousts and gifts from the new knights to their friends.

But first, they spend the whole night praying. They do not eat or sleep all night—only pray that God will help them in their new duties.

When dawn breaks, they bath and dress in long white robes. This shows that they promise to be pure and faithful.

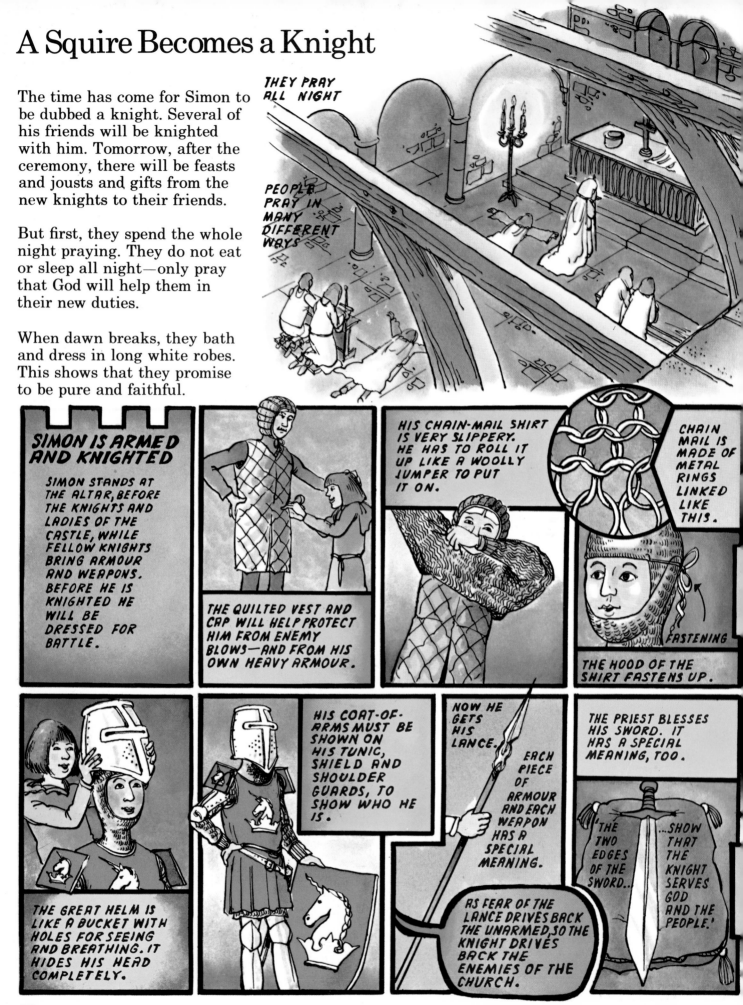

THEY PRAY ALL NIGHT

PEOPLE PRAY IN MANY DIFFERENT WAYS

SIMON IS ARMED AND KNIGHTED

SIMON STANDS AT THE ALTAR, BEFORE THE KNIGHTS AND LADIES OF THE CASTLE, WHILE FELLOW KNIGHTS BRING ARMOUR AND WEAPONS. BEFORE HE IS KNIGHTED HE WILL BE DRESSED FOR BATTLE.

THE QUILTED VEST AND CAP WILL HELP PROTECT HIM FROM ENEMY BLOWS—AND FROM HIS OWN HEAVY ARMOUR.

HIS CHAIN-MAIL SHIRT IS VERY SLIPPERY. HE HAS TO ROLL IT UP LIKE A WOOLLY JUMPER TO PUT IT ON.

CHAIN MAIL IS MADE OF METAL RINGS LINKED LIKE THIS.

FASTENING

THE HOOD OF THE SHIRT FASTENS UP.

THE GREAT HELM IS LIKE A BUCKET WITH HOLES FOR SEEING AND BREATHING. IT HIDES HIS HEAD COMPLETELY.

HIS COAT-OF-ARMS MUST BE SHOWN ON HIS TUNIC, SHIELD AND SHOULDER GUARDS, TO SHOW WHO HE IS.

NOW HE GETS HIS LANCE.

EACH PIECE OF ARMOUR AND EACH WEAPON HAS A SPECIAL MEANING.

AS FEAR OF THE LANCE DRIVES BACK THE UNARMED, SO THE KNIGHT DRIVES BACK THE ENEMIES OF THE CHURCH.

THE PRIEST BLESSES HIS SWORD. IT HAS A SPECIAL MEANING, TOO.

'THE TWO EDGES OF THE SWORD... ...SHOW THAT THE KNIGHT SERVES GOD AND THE PEOPLE.'

AT DAWN THEY BATH AND DRESS.

THE CHEST PROTECTOR IS A NEW KIND OF ARMOUR, MADE OF METAL PLATES.

THE LEGS OF A MOUNTED KNIGHT ARE AN EASY TARGET, SO HE WEARS METAL SHIN-GUARDS AS WELL AS MAIL LEGGINGS.

SHINGUARDS
LEGGINGS

THE ARM GUARDS AND SHOULDER GUARDS ARE TO SHIELD HIM FROM SLASHING SIDE-BLOWS.

THE TUNIC IS TO KEEP HIS ARMOUR FROM RUSTING IN THE RAIN AND SUN.

NOW BARON GODFREY GIVES SIMON THE KISS OF PEACE. THEN HE STRIKES HIM WITH THE FLAT OF THE SWORD.

AWAKE FROM EVIL DREAMS AND KEEP WATCH, FAITHFUL IN CHRIST AND PRAISEWORTHY IN FAME.

SIMON HAS BEEN DUBBED A KNIGHT.

NOW SIMON GETS HIS SPURS. HOLDING HIS SWORD, HE THINKS OF THE SWORDS OF THE GREAT HEROES — JOYEAUX, THE SWORD OF CHARLEMAGNE — EXCALIBUR, THE SWORD OF ARTHUR.

IT IS SIMON HIMSELF WHO KNIGHTS HIS GREAT FRIEND GERALD. THIS IS ONE OF HIS PRIVILEGES, NOW HE IS A KNIGHT.

AND NOW... ON TO THE FEASTS AND THE JOUSTING!

23

At the Scene of a Joust

Baron Godfrey has arranged a tournament celebrate Simon's knighthood. The sun blaz on the lists—the fenced-off place where the knights will joust. Trumpets blare, to announce the arrival of the strange Black Knight. Simon has challenged him.

Today, for the first time, Simon has the chance to prove his skill in the joust—like his father and uncles, and like Roland and Richard Lion Heart in the minstrels' stories

ARMS OF VON RAPPARD (RAPPE MEANS BLACK HORSE)

ARMS OF VON BAUM (BAUM MEANS TREE)

CITY ARMS OF LOWEN (LÖWE MEANS LION)

CITY ARMS OF AHLEN (AHLEN MEANS EEL)

ARMS OF VON BRUNN (BRUNNEN MEANS WELL)

ALE HOUSE

This lady is the queen of the joust. She was chosen, as the best and most elegant of the ladies, to give the prize to the best knight.

PIE SELLER

LADY ANNA

TRUMPETERS

QUEEN OF LOVE AND BEAUTY

HERALD

The herald announce the contestants and recounts their great deeds. He must be ab to recognize everyon from their coats-of- a

This glove was given to Simon by his cousin Anna. It shows he is her favourite knight. He hopes to bring honour to her—he thinks she is the sweetest and merriest lady he knows.

LADY'S FAVOUR

SIMON

HIGH POMME

ROBERT

When he became a knight, Simon vowed to protect the poor and honour women. Today he is wondering if he is skilful and strong enough to keep his vow.

Notice the high-pommelled saddle that has come into fashion. Now it is almost impossible to unhorse your opponent.

THIS IS A PICK-POCKET

THIS IS A POCKET

ON THE FIRST CHARGE, SIMON'S LANCE IS SHATTERED. BUT EACH KNIGHT CAN LOSE THREE LANCES BEFORE HE IS DEFEATED.

SIMON MEETS THE BLACK KNIGHT

THE TRUMPETS SOUND THE CHARGE, AND SIMON DIGS IN HIS SPURS. IF HE STRIKES THE CREST OF THE BLACK KNIGHT'S HELM, HE WILL WIN HIS FIRST POINT.

The field is crowded. People come from miles around—some to prove their skill, some to show their beauty, some just to enjoy the sports and feasts in the nearby fairground.

Simon's cousin Robert is at his side. He will arm Simon, rub down his horse, and come to his aid if he is injured—just as Simon did, when he was a young squire. Below you can see what happens when Simon meets his foe.

Coats-of-arms

An armoured knight has to wear a special sign on his shield and armour to show who he is. This is called a 'coat-of-arms'. At first these were simple. A knight picked almost any design he liked—perhaps a splendid beast or a picture that showed what his name meant. You can see some of them here.

Most people have only one name, like Simon, but they often have nicknames—like Simon from Strong Mountain ('Montfort' in French). Some coats-of-arms show these.

The ladies and nobles watch the jousts from splendid tents. They like jousts much more than tourneys which are muddled and brutal. In a tourney, two armies charge each other. There is blood and dust and noise. Men may be wounded and even killed.

DYING KNIGHT

The Black Knight is a knight errant. Most of his father's lands went to his elder brother, so he seeks his fortune at jousts. If he wins he gets the horse and armour of his foe. If he takes a rich knight prisoner he may get ransom money.

The young squires wait and watch, to see if they are needed. If a knight falls, only his own squire may help him.

SQUIRES

This knight was defeated in this morning's joust. He has lost his horse and armour, and he has spent his last penny to pay his faithful squire. Now he has nothing.

WOUNDED KNIGHT

DEFEATED KNIGHT

GRIFFIN WITH CROWN

SEA-HORSE

UNICORN

PEGASUS

ON THE LAST CHARGE, THE LANCES OF BOTH MEN ARE SMASHED. THEY DISMOUNT, TO CONTINUE THE DUEL WITH SWORDS.

AND THE BLACK KNIGHT IS DOWN. HE IS NOW AT SIMON'S MERCY. HE CAN BE STRIPPED OF HIS ARMOUR AND HELD PRISONER TILL RANSOMED.

BUT SIMON RELEASES HIM. HIS ONLY REQUEST IS TO EXCHANGE HORSES WITH HIS BRAVE FOE, AS A REMINDER OF THIS GREAT BATTLE.

Return From the Crusades

One day, a strange procession appears at the castle gates. Tanned, weary-looking men lead a ragged string of mules and donkeys, laden with baggage. Among the pack-animals is a creature none of the castle people have seen before. Everyone runs to look. Even the men look strange. There is something foreign about their clothes and saddlery.

It is hard at first for Lady Alice to recognize that one of these men is her brother Rudolf—back from his travels on crusade. He has been away for four years.

Below you can find out where the crusaders went and what they did.

What is a Crusade?

A crusade is a religious war. The most famous crusades, in the time of knights and castles, were wars in which Christian armies from Europe tried to conquer Jerusalem and the holy places where Jesus lived and died. Like all wars, of course, they really happened for more than one reason. They started in 1095.

For centuries, Christians had made pilgrimages to the Holy Land – the bit marked in red on this map.

For a long time, the pilgrims were treated well by the Arabs who ruled the Holy Land. The Arabs had a different religion (they followed the teachings of the Prophet Mohammed), but they were very courteous people. They respected the beliefs of the Christians, and made them welcome.

However, in the 11th century, the Arabs were conquered by the Seldjuk Turks. Now the map looked like this. (Notice how the red of the Arab states has been eaten up by the green that marks the Turkish states.)

The Turks were also Moslems (followers of Mohammed), but they felt less sympathetic to the Christians. They made life hard for them, making them pay vast sums of money to see the holy city of Jerusalem.

Meanwhile, the people of Europe had really begun to want the goods that were brought from the Holy Land –particularly spices, which they used to preserve their food for the winter. So they were, for many reasons, very angry with the Turks.

When the head of the Christian church, Pope Urban II in Rome, demanded that they fight for Jerusalem, they were ready. This was the First Crusade.

The crusades continued for over two hundred years. Jerusalem was won by the Christians and then lost again. The map changed many times. In the end, Jerusalem stayed in the hands of the Moslems. But as you can see, the goods and stories brought back by the crusaders changed life for all Europe.

The Castle is Attacked

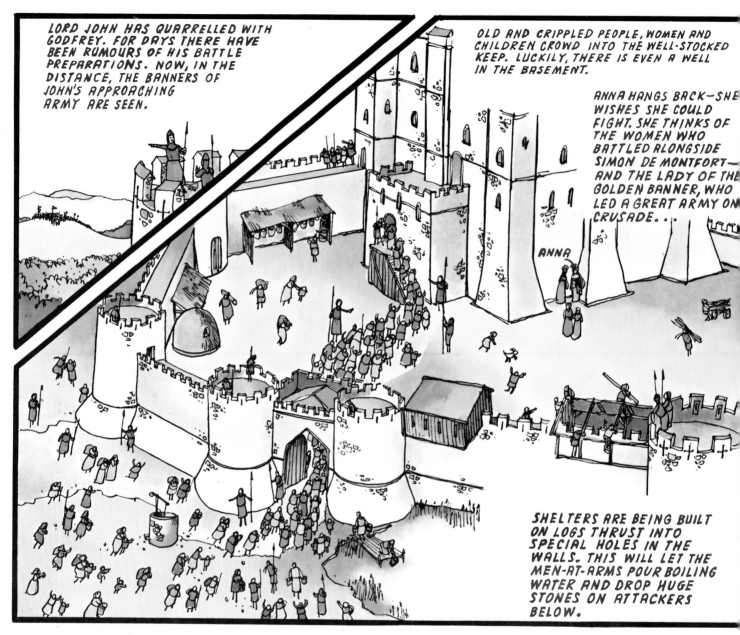

LORD JOHN HAS QUARRELLED WITH GODFREY. FOR DAYS THERE HAVE BEEN RUMOURS OF HIS BATTLE PREPARATIONS. NOW, IN THE DISTANCE, THE BANNERS OF JOHN'S APPROACHING ARMY ARE SEEN.

OLD AND CRIPPLED PEOPLE, WOMEN AND CHILDREN CROWD INTO THE WELL-STOCKED KEEP. LUCKILY, THERE IS EVEN A WELL IN THE BASEMENT.

ANNA HANGS BACK—SHE WISHES SHE COULD FIGHT. SHE THINKS OF THE WOMEN WHO BATTLED ALONGSIDE SIMON DE MONTFORT—AND THE LADY OF THE GOLDEN BANNER, WHO LED A GREAT ARMY ON CRUSADE...

ANNA

SHELTERS ARE BEING BUILT ON LOGS THRUST INTO SPECIAL HOLES IN THE WALLS. THIS WILL LET THE MEN-AT-ARMS POUR BOILING WATER AND DROP HUGE STONES ON ATTACKERS BELOW.

Siege Weapons

Often the most powerful weapons in a siege are food and water. If the besiegers are well-supplied and the castle is not, the besiegers can just sit back and wait. Sooner or later the defenders must starve or surrender. At other times the besiegers might give up—from bad food, illness, or boredom.

Both sides use other weapons to try to win more quickly— like the siege machines shown here. Most of these were used long ago by the Romans.

If the besiegers fill in the ditch round the castle, they can do lots of damage. For instance, they can roll a siege tower against the wall, raise its platform, and climb in.

SIEGE TOWER

Or they can tunnel under the wall and then burn the wooden props of the tunnel, so that the wall collapses.

IT IS NOON OF THE SECOND DAY. LORD JOHN'S MEN HAVE TUNNELLED UNDER THE CASTLE WALL. THE WALL CRUMBLES. THE DEFENDERS RETREAT.

IT IS NIGHT. UNKNOWN TO THE ENEMY, SIMON AND A GROUP OF KNIGHTS CREPT OUT OF A SECRET GATE (THE POSTERN GATE) AT THE BACK OF THE CASTLE. SILENTLY, THEY SET FIRE TO THE ENEMIES' SUPPLIES. THE ENEMY FLEES!

MANY HAVE DIED. EVEN BARON GODFREY HAS BEEN WOUNDED. BUT THE CASTLE IS SAVED.

They can batter down the wall with heavy logs or special battering rams.

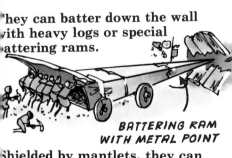

BATTERING RAM WITH METAL POINT

Shielded by mantlets, they can bring scaling ladders and try to climb the wall.

MANTLET

Most archers use cross-bows. A cross-bow takes a long time to load. You must use a winch—or two hands and a foot.

WINCH

STIRRUP

ARROW SLITS FOR CROSS-BOW

The English have learned to use long-bows. These can be shot much more quickly.

ARROW SLITS FOR LONG-BOW

Castle Map

This map shows where you can find some of the best-preserved examples of castles built about the time the events in this book take place.

FINLAND

NORWAY   SWEDEN

⚔Abo

Akershus

⚔Visby

DENMARK

RUSSIA

⚔Hammershus

⚔Marienburg

Drum⚔

⚔Craigmillar
Alnwick

Carrickfergus⚔

IRELAND   BRITAIN

Trim⚔

⚔Conisbrough

POLAND

⚔Caernarvon
Carlow⚔ ⚔Harlech
Ferns

HOLLAND   WEST GERMANY

⚔Castle Rising

EAST GERMANY

Leyden ⚔Muiden

⚔Chepstow Tower
of London

⚔Chateau des Comtes

⚔Restormel

BELGIUM

Marksburg⚔

⚔Coburg

⚔Bezdéz

⚔Eltz

⚔Karlstejn

⚔Arques

CZECHOSLOVAKIA

Chateau Gaillard ⚔Gisors
La Roche Guyon⚔

Falkenstein⚔

LUXEMBOURG

⚔Ortenberg
⚔Araberg

⚔Etampes

AUSTRIA

⚔Viechtenstein

HUNGARY

Angers⚔
Langeais⚔ ⚔Loches

⚔Pfeffengen

RUMANIA

SWITZERLAND

⚔Kropfenstein

FRANCE

⚔Chillon

⚔Trento

Fenis⚔ Sirmione⚔

Golubac⚔

⚔Castelvecchio

⚔Villandraut

⚔Gradara

YUGOSLAVIA

Aigues Mortes

San Gimignano

Carcassonne⚔

Sarzanello

BULGARIA

ITALY

⚔Burgos

ALBANIA

⚔Castel Sant' Angelo

⚔Villalonso

Castel del Monte

Roumeli Hissar⚔

⚔Avila

⚔Castel Nuovo

Anadoli Hissar

⚔Amieira

SPAIN

SARDINIA

GREECE

⚔Lisbon

PORTUGAL

Bellver

Palermo⚔

Monte Agudo⚔

⚔Catania

SICILY

CRETE

ALGERIA   TUNISIA

MOROCCO

30

How Castles Grew

A castle is a fortress you can live in, protected from your enemies. The first kind of castle in Europe (before about 1000 AD) was a low tower, usually two stories high, with the living hall above the storerooms.

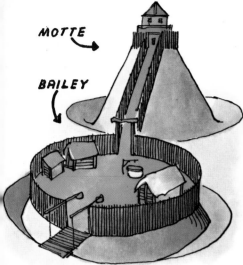

MOTTE

BAILEY

When people had to build quickly, as the Normans did after they conquered England, they sometimes built castles of wood. They often used a motte-and-bailey castle.

As you can see, the 'motte' is a mound. The 'bailey' is a fenced-off place that holds up invaders. Sometimes these were later replaced by stone castles.

TURKEY

SYRIA

★Krak des Chevaliers

CYPRUS

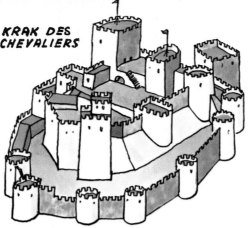

KRAK DES CHEVALIERS

The crusaders learned a lot about castle-building from the great castles they found on crusades, like the famous Krak des Chevaliers, in Syria.

CAERPHILLY

After this, many castles were built with several circles of walls (concentric castles) or other improvements, like towers along the walls (mural towers).

Castles grew a little differently in each place. For example, in mountainous parts of Italy, a castle might be just a tower built on a rocky peak.

COUCY

In France, many castles became luxurious homes for noblemen. Castles built by the Teutonic Knights of Germany had chapels within their walls.

And each castle, in each country, has its own special story.

Useful Dates

When you read history, it is useful to keep some dates in mind to help work out why certain happenings were important. These dates may help.

1 AD Birth of Jesus
AD (anno Domini) means 'Year of our Lord'. When our calendar was started, people thought Jesus was born in this year. At this time, the Romans ruled all round the Mediterranean Sea and in parts of Europe.

476 Fall of Rome
Warriors from the north had been fighting the Romans for centuries. At last they destroyed Rome.

732 Defeat of the Moslems by Charles Martel
The next conquering people round the Mediterranean were the Moslems. They conquered Portugal and Spain, but Charles Martel defeated them in France.

870 Danish Conquest Begins
Vikings from Denmark had been raiding Europe for years. Now they started colonies. Many of the ideas of knighthood were started by Europeans defending themselves against the Vikings.

1066 Norman Conquest
Vikings who had settled in Normandy (France) conquered Britain.

1095 First Crusade Begins
European Christians tried to conquer Jerusalem.

1150 First Paper Mill in Europe. Universities started (Paris and Salerno)
The crusaders brought back many inventions and ideas from the Moslems, who had big libraries, and universities where people exchanged knowledge.

1380 Bible Translated into English.
Until about this time, few ordinary people had a chance to read the Bible. When they did, many began to protest against the priests (argue that they were wrong). They became known as Protestants.

Going Further

Looking at Castles

At good bookshops you can buy maps of your area that show any nearby castles or castle remains. Try Ordnance Survey (1 to 50,000) or Bartholomews (1 to 100,000) maps.

To find the best castles, though, you need a guide book. *The Castles of England*, by Frederick Wilkinson (Letts Guides) has good descriptions of many castles, and also photographs and drawings. *Historic Houses, Castles and Gardens* (ABC Historic Publication) has lots of information on castles, including opening hours, prices, and how to get there.

When you visit a castle, notice things like rivers and ditches and how the ground slopes, to work out where an enemy would attack. Sometimes you can only guess what the castle would have been like, long ago. Look for clues—like holes for beams in the walls.

Looking at Churches

Ask at libraries and tourist offices to find interesting old churches. On the arms of some very old choir stalls you can still see the scratch-marks where choir-boys once played games like draughts. Turn-up seats in choirs sometimes have very funny and interesting carvings underneath. Also, notice the dates carved in Roman numerals on the walls and grave-stones.

Books to Read

Look in the library for fact books, but try these books, too. The first three are paperbacks.
King Arthur and His Knights of the Round Table by Roger Lancelyn Green (Puffin)
The Adventures of Robin Hood by Roger Lancelyn Green (Puffin)
The Sword and the Stone by T. H. White (Armada Lion)
The Story of Mankind by Hendrik Van Loop (Harrap)

Consultants

Peter Vansittart is a novelist with a special interest in the 13th century. He is a former teacher and a distinguished writer on historical subjects.

Angela Littler has written and edited several best-selling children's information books.

Nicholas Hall specializes in medieval architecture, armour and weapons.

Gillian Evans is with the Medieval Centre at Reading University.

We would like to thank the Western Manuscript Department of the Bodleian Library at Oxford for permission to reproduce material from their collection on pages 4 and 5.

Index

The name Usborne and the device are Trade Marks of Usborne Publishing Ltd.

proost
INTERNATIONAL BOOK PRODUCTION
PRINTED IN BELGIUM BY